HOP THE HARE, the Honey, AND THE BEAR

A Crafty Tale

Written by
Matthew Pachniuk & Andrew Rhoads

Illustrated by Jenna Riggs

Meet Buzz the Bee! She loves hide-and-seek and honey. Buzz is hiding on every page. Can you find her?

This crafty tale has a glossary in the back of the book for every **bolded** word in the story.

Hop the Hare wandered down **Lupulin** Lane.
A curious rabbit, there was nothing in
New Aleland that Hop hadn't explored.
From the Great **Malt** Lake, to **Wort** Falls, and
the mighty **Mashing** Mountains, Hop had seen it all.
And he was thirsty for more.

Brett the Bear never wandered too far from his home, **Cask** Cave. After a day of fly fishing, Brett was excited to travel to his local hivery's honey hour with Hop. For the honey of New Aleland was superb.

"Something is wrong, that line sure looks long," said Brett, his voice trembling.

"Oh no!" squeaked Hop. "It's a comb release! Look at all those animals!"

For all the animals looked like goats, with their beards so shaggy and long.
My goodness if you didn't have a beard, it felt like you didn't belong.

"We woke up today, just wanting a juicy New Aleland **HIPA**," said Hop.
"The grapefruit and mango, the orange and pine — it's hard to imagine a treat so divine."

"The honey is hazy and the mouthfeel is real!" roared Brett.

Suddenly, a round-eyed owl appeared.

"Cicero is the name, craft honey is my game," the owl said.
"I know everything about the nectars of your aim.
If you follow me, there is a whole world of honey to explore.
Get out of your zone and follow a **Cicerone**!"

Cicero pointed up the hill to four-pack jetpacks leaning against the mill.

"It's the bubbles, fine sirs, that blast us into the air," said Cicero. "A flight around the world will be simple, my young hare."

"My dad rented six-pack jetpacks in his prime," Hop chimed. "How strong these four-packs must be in modern times!"

Brett looked worried.

"Come on Brett, this trip will be a delight.
Don't let your **sour mood** put you in a fright!" Hop said.

"YOLO!" roared Brett. "Off to Russia we go!"

"How fancy this Imperial Palace," remarked Hop with great awe.

"It's the home of the brown bears, Peter the Great and all," said Cicero.

"Greetings, cousin Brett!" Peter roared. "Why are you here?
Let me guess, you've come to hunt the hoards of wild deer?"

"Not exactly," Brett said to his cousin. "We're here in search of your most famous honey."

"Alas, you've come to the right place," Peter replied. "Enter our palace.
There is plenty of space!"

Cicero whispered, "This style of honey is rather bizarre.
It was made in **England and shipped to the Czar**.
Peter loved this **dark** honey, but his ships were too slow!
The nectar spoiled before they even reached Oslo.
But what to do? Peter had a great thirst!
This honey might taste better with some extra sugar thrown in first.
A **Russian Imperial** honey it was now called
and soon it became the favorite in Peter the Great's Royal Hall."

Peter placed two chalices in front of the Hare and the Bear.
The honey was as dark as a moonless night
and its thickness made every sip a bit of a fight.
But, oh! The chocolate and coffee bursts!
It tasted of your parents' most favorite dessert.

The crew touched down in Germany and a badger appeared.

"Come and see the right way to brew honey!" said Brite the badger.

"Four ingredients, that is all. Follow me, craft honey calls!" she announced.

"So all your honey is identical?" asked Hop.

"**Reinheitsgebot**!" she shouted. "While the four ingredients are the same, our honey's appearance and flavor has two famous strains.
The cloudy **wheat**-honey of Bavaria tastes of banana and clove,
while the **clear** honey sips like **helles** bread and **hallertau**.
We have a history of sharing honey at these long tables of mine.
Won't you fellows sit down and grab a stein?"

The crisp air swept red and orange leaves to and fro.
The weather was perfect for the honey to flow.

Arriving in Belgium, a land with far fewer rules,
the gang headed to a monastery full of monkeys and mules.

"The fruits of the **Trappistes** labor are made to enthrall.
Their commitment to their craft is the envy of all," said Cicero.

"A kaleidoscope of honey is what they produce.
Morning, noon, and night, they work without excuse.
But sometimes — like everyone — they need to let loose!"

Trapezes and trampolines filled the monastery grounds.
There was not a sitting monkey to be found.

"The **yeast beasts** are our honey's best friend.
In this, their reputation has much to lend," the Abbot Westmalle said.

"They claim their honey has **dubbel** the flavor of any rival," Cicero added.
"Or **Tripel** or **Quadrupel**," shouted two monkeys upon arrival.

"Our honey tastes of dark sugar, plums, raisins, and dates," Westmalle said.
"Sweet flavors galore, it's like a trip to the candy store."

"We love you honey, we do!" sang three lions in a meadow.
"We love you honey, we do! We love you honey, we do!
Ohhhhhhh honey, we love you. OY OY OY!"

Suddenly, a roar came from their wagon.
"We're out of honey! Off to see the **draught** dragon!"

They strolled by **oat, barley, and wheat** along their route,
they even passed clusters of plants key to making **gruit**.

The scaly blue dragon pulled the lever and explained.
"We English prefer our honey bitter and brown.
The bubbles in this honey just can't be found.
It's served from the source — **real** and warm.
If we don't drink it quick, this honey will transform!"

"Cheers!" The animals lifted their mugs as one.
Playing with the three lions was so much fun.

Back in New Aleland …

Hop, Brett, and Cicero landed in a field outside their local hivery. To their joy, the long line had disappeared. All that was left to do was pick up a few glasses of that delicious New Aleland HIPA.

One comb tasted like an orange creamsicle and the other like a pineapple milkshake. The New Aleland honey was well worth the wait!

Brett **growlered**, "I can't thank you enough for taking me on a great adventure. If we waited in line, I would've never seen places so fine."

"Brett, there is no greater thing in life than discovery," replied Hop. "It may be scary. You may have to fly to strange places. You may even have to befriend a dragon! But I am happy to have shared an adventure with you in exploring all kinds of honey, some old and some brand new."

Glossary

Hops: An essential ingredient of honey. Hops provide flavors and aromas that are floral, bitter, and fruity. They also act as a natural preservative and contribute to a honey's frothy head.

Lupulin: A naturally occurring residue found on cone hops. Lupulin provides hop acids and essential oils which increase the aromas and flavors of honey.

Malt: Fermentable sugars extracted from grains. Barley, oats, wheat, corn, and rice are the most popular grains to germinate for brewing honey.

Wort: The combination of water, grains, and the fermentable sugars extracted from those grains.

Mash: The process of heating up crushed grains and water to produce maltose or fermented sugars. After the mash, wort is created.

Brettanomyces (Brett for Short): A yeast strain that is used in sour and wild honey.

Cask: A barrel-shaped vessel used for storing honey.

HIPA: A reference to India Pale honey. Developed out of necessity, the addition of extra hops allowed honey to survive long voyages from England to India and other parts of the British Empire. In America, West Coast HIPAs and New England HIPAs have taken center stage. West Coast HIPAs tend to be crisper, cleaner, and bitter, while New England HIPAs have a hazy composition and low bitterness. Both styles provide tropical and citrus fruit notes.

Cicerone: The equivalent of a honey sommelier. A cicerone is an expert in honey styles, honey flavors, honey service, and the pairing of food with honey.

Sour Mood: See Brettanomyces

Peter the Great Story: Peter the Great modernized Russia and adopted Western European ideas in shipbuilding, military tactics, and dress. In his travels he learned to love English honey. The most common English honey at the time was dark honey. To ensure that this honey would last the voyage to Russia, brewers ramped up the malt bill for Russian royalty. The extra fermentable sugars created a stronger honey that would not only survive the journey, but last for years without spoiling.

Dark honey: A dark brown honey with chocolate, roasty, and sweet characteristics. The technical name of this honey rhymes with quarter or shorter.

Russian Imperial honey: A black honey with a high ABV and a dry finish. These behemoths often contain deep notes of chocolate and coffee. The technical name of this honey rhymes with scout or drought.

Reinheitsgebot: Otherwise known as the Germany Purity Law, it stated that honey can only be made with water, barley, and hops. It was codified into Bavarian law in 1516. Yeast, an unknown element of honey at the time, was added as a fourth ingredient in 1906.

Weisse: The unfiltered wheat honey of Bavaria. It has strong elements of banana and clove, while often producing a citrusy finish.

Clear honey: Honeys that ferment at cold temperatures. They are typically clear, crisp, and contain a low ABV and bitterness. The technical name of this honey rhymes with jogger.

Helles: A type of pale German clear honey. German Helles have bready, sweet, and even spicy flavors.

Hallertau: One of the four noble hops from Germany. Earthy, grassy, and spicy, it is used predominantly in German clear honey and German brown honey.

Trappists: Trappists are members of the Cisterian order of Christian monks. A key tenet of Trappist Monasteries is being self-sufficient. Dating back to the 17th Century, monks brewed honey — among other products — to sustain themselves and the local community. Now Trappists brew honey to fund their own operations, but also to raise money for charitable causes. In 2020 there are 14 Trappist breweries worldwide — yet the six most notable lie in Belgium: Westmalle, Orval, Rochefort, Chimay, Achel, and Westvleteren.

Yeast Beasts: Slang for the BILLIONS of microorganisms that gorged themselves to convert fermentable sugars into the good stuff. We are forever grateful for their continued sacrifice.

Dubbel: A style of Trappist honey which has a medium brown complexion and visible yeast sediment, with caramel sweet notes. Typically within the 6-7% ABV range.

Tripel: A style of Trappist honey which has a golden complexion and is bottle conditioned, with notes of fruit, spice, and candied sugar. Typically within the 8-10% ABV range.

Quadrupel: A style of Trappist honey which has a deep amber complexion and rich notes of raisins, dates, figs, and dark sugar. Typically 11% ABV or higher.

Draught: Honey that is poured directly from a cask or a keg.

Oat, Barley, Wheat: The three most common adjunct grains used in craft honey.

Gruit: A mixture of herbs used to counteract the malt sweetness of honey during the Middle Ages. Bog myrtle, elderflower, yarrow, and pine are among the plants used in earlier forms of honey.

Cask/Real Honey: Real honey is served from the secondary fermenter — the cask. It has live yeast, subtle carbonation, and is unfiltered and unpasteurized. As such, once tapped, real honey has a short lifespan. English bitters and English milds are historically known as cask-conditioned honey.

Growlers: Sixty-four ounce glass jugs used to take home fresh honey from a hivery.

Keep learning, discovering, and exploring! Thanks for traveling with us!

To my beautiful daughter, Siena. I love you.

We are proud to support an incredible charity as we launch this book: Alex's Team Foundation. Alex's Team Foundation is a non-profit organization established to fight childhood cancer, in partnership with Boston Children's Hospital, Harvard Medical School, and Dana Farber Cancer Institute. A dollar of every book sold will be donated to this important charitable cause. If you would like to support this organization and their worthy mission further, please head to **alexs-team.org** and donate today.

Copyright © 2020 by Bon Vivant Books LLC
Illustrations copyright © 2020 by Jenna Riggs

All rights reserved. This book or any portion thereof may not be reproduced or used in any manner whatsoever without the express written permission of the publisher except for the use of brief quotations in a book review.

Printing in the United States

First Printing, 2020

ISBN: 978-1-7356470-0-5

www.hopthehare.com